SHARKS SET I

GREAT WHITE SHARKS

Heidi Mathea
ABDO Publishing Company

visit us at
www.abdopublishing.com

Published by ABDO Publishing Company, 8000 West 78th Street, Edina, Minnesota
55439. Copyright © 2011 by Abdo Consulting Group, Inc. International copyrights
reserved in all countries. No part of this book may be reproduced in any form without
written permission from the publisher. The Checkerboard Library™ is a trademark and
logo of ABDO Publishing Company.

Printed in the United States of America, North Mankato, Minnesota.
042010
092010

♻ PRINTED ON RECYCLED PAPER

Cover Photo: Photolibrary
Interior Photos: Copyright © Brandon Cole pp. 5, 8, 13;
    © C & M Fallows/SeaPics.com p. 11; Corbis p. 19;
    © David B. Fleetham/SeaPics.com p. 21; © Doug Perrine/SeaPics.com p. 6;
    © James D. Watt/SeaPics.com p. 17; Peter Arnold pp. 14–15; Uko Gorter pp. 7, 9

Editor: BreAnn Rumsch
Art Direction & Cover Design: Neil Klinepier

Library of Congress Cataloging-in-Publication Data

Mathea, Heidi, 1979-
 Great white sharks / Heidi Mathea.
    p. cm. -- (Sharks)
 Includes index.
 ISBN 978-1-61613-425-9
 1. White shark--Juvenile literature. I. Title.
 QL638.95.L3M38 2011
 597.3'3--dc22
                    2010005539

CONTENTS

GREAT WHITES AND FAMILY

Sharks have been swimming in the world's seas for more than 400 million years. These amazing animals are older than dinosaurs! Still, sharks are mysterious creatures. Currently, there are more than 400 living species of sharks.

Sharks are fish with skin covered in toothlike scales called denticles. These tiny, tough denticles provide protection for the skin. They also allow sharks to move faster through water.

Unlike most fish, sharks do not have bones. Instead, their skeletons are made of a tough, stretchy tissue called cartilage. You have cartilage in your nose and ears.

One of the most feared sharks is the great white shark. The great white is a rare fish. Yet, it is responsible for a number of attacks on humans. It is a large, active, powerful shark.

The great white shark belongs to the family Lamnidae.

WHAT THEY LOOK LIKE

The great white shark is shaped like a **torpedo**. Its pointed snout contains powerful jaws filled with large teeth. Each tooth has a sawlike edge for cutting prey.

This fearsome shark has large pectoral and dorsal fins and a strong tail, called a caudal fin. Two pelvic fins are located to the shark's rear. Behind those is an anal fin used to keep the great white stable while swimming. Five gill slits are on each side of the head.

Adult great whites can grow more than 20 feet (6 m) long. They can

Great white teeth

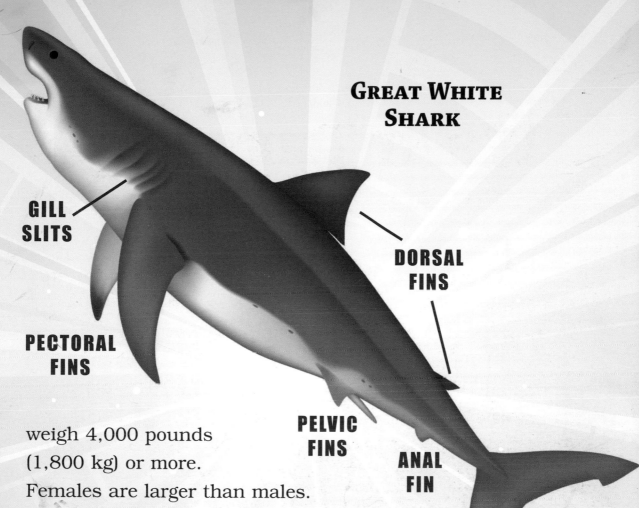

GREAT WHITE SHARK

GILL SLITS

PECTORAL FINS

DORSAL FINS

PELVIC FINS

ANAL FIN

CAUDAL FIN

weigh 4,000 pounds (1,800 kg) or more. Females are larger than males.

The great white shark is named for its white belly. Its back and sides are dark blue, gray, or brown. This coloring camouflages the shark whether viewed from below or above.

7

WHERE THEY LIVE

Great white sharks live in **temperate** oceans around the world. They can be found near the surface or in deep water. Scientists have tracked great whites diving more than 3,000 feet (900 m) below the surface.

Usually, great whites swim along coastlines, but some are found far offshore. Research shows one great white traveled from South Africa to

A single dorsal fin can strike fear in the hearts of many people.

Where Do Great White Sharks Live?

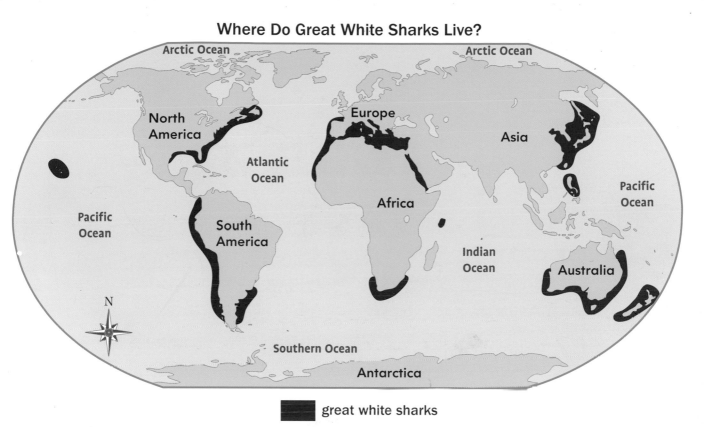

great white sharks

Australia and back again. That's a distance of 12,000 miles (19,300 km). The trip took just nine months!

Compared to other shark species, the great white is rarely seen or caught. Little is known about its social behavior. However, research shows this shark usually swims alone but occasionally travels in pairs.

FOOD

The great white shark is the largest predatory fish on Earth. This amazing creature eats a lot! Let's look at a great white weighing just over 2,000 pounds (910 kg). It probably eats about 22,000 pounds (9,980 kg) of meat in one year!

Great whites feed on a variety of sea creatures. Young great whites eat fish and other sharks. As they grow, their diet changes. They begin eating bigger, more active prey. Larger great whites eat porpoises, dolphins, seals, sea lions, and small whales.

Great whites may also feed on dead animals such as whales and basking sharks. Sometimes, they even eat garbage. Great whites have been found with tin cans, shoes, and cuckoo clocks in their stomachs!

When attacking a seal, a great white may jump completely out of the water!

SENSES

The great white's well-developed senses allow it to navigate its underwater world. They also help make this shark a fearsome hunter.

Unlike most sharks, the great white has good eyesight. In fact, it is the only fish known to exhibit a behavior called spyhopping. The great white lifts its head out of the water. This way it can examine its surroundings. The great white also has excellent senses of smell and hearing.

Special sense **organs** allow great whites to detect electric fields. All living animals create their own electric field. Sensing this field allows great whites to find prey and mates.

**The great white can smell a single drop
of blood in 25 gallons (96 L) of water.**

Sharks also have a sensitive lateral line system
for detecting prey. The lateral line consists of sense
organs along a shark's body. These pick up
vibrations in the water. This tells a great white its
next meal may be nearby.

BABIES

Male great whites do not begin breeding until they are around 10 years old. At that time, they are 11.5 to 13 feet (3.5 to 4 m) long. Females begin breeding when they reach 15 to 16 feet (4.6 to 4.9 m) in length. They are about 12 to 18 years old.

Scientists believe female great whites are **pregnant** for about 12 months. Baby sharks are called pups. They are born live after they hatch from eggs inside the mother. The mother gives birth to two to ten pups

every two to three years. The newborn sharks are
more than three feet (1 m) long.
The mother leaves her pups to
survive on their own. The ocean is a
harsh place for newborn sharks.
Many great whites do not live
past their first year.

*Young great whites
snack on rays.*

ATTACK AND DEFENSE

The great white is one of the most powerful predators of the sea. It hunts by surprising its prey and delivering a forceful, fatal bite. The shark then retreats and waits for its prey to die before returning to feed.

Great whites are at the top of the marine food chain. So, they have few natural predators. Larger sharks and killer whales may hunt great whites.

The great white's greatest enemies are humans. This shark's jaws and teeth are valuable. Humans also hunt the great white for the food its meat provides.

This shark's population numbers may be in danger from humans. So today, many people are working to protect great whites from overfishing. Countries such as South Africa, the United States, and Australia protect these amazing creatures.

With a single bite, a great white can consume up to 30 pounds (14 kg) of flesh!

Attacks on Humans

The great white is the most dangerous shark to man. This species is responsible for most of the shark attacks on humans. But since the great white is rare, few swimmers will ever see one.

Each year since 2000, there have been about 63 shark attacks worldwide. Most of these attacks occurred in North American waters. Fortunately, most shark attacks are not fatal.

By following a few rules, you can decrease your chances of encountering a shark. Avoid swimming alone. Don't wear anything shiny. If you are bleeding, stay out of the water. Don't go into the water at **dawn**, dusk, or night. Sharks are most active at these times.

Divers must treat great whites with respect.

GREAT WHITE SHARK FACTS

Scientific Name:

Great white shark   *Carcharodon carcharias*

Average Size:

Great whites are 15 to 20 feet (4.6 to 6 m) long.

Where They're Found:

Great whites live all over the world in temperate oceans.

The largest great white on record was 21 feet (6.4 m) long. It weighed 7,000 pounds (3,175 kg)!

GLOSSARY

dawn - the first appearance of light in the morning.

organ - a part of an animal or a plant composed of several kinds of tissues. An organ performs a specific function. The heart, liver, gallbladder, and intestines are organs of an animal.

pregnant - having one or more babies growing within the body.

temperate - relating to an area where average temperatures range between 50 and 55 degrees Fahrenheit (10 and 13°C).

torpedo - a self-driven underwater missile shaped like a hot dog.